Sprint Car Racing
Unleashing the Power

By Susan Sexton

Perfection Learning®

Designers: Emily J. Greazel and Nancy Suits
Illustrator: Dea Marks: pp. 14, 32

Image Credits:
Roland Miraco: Cover, pp. 3, 6, 7, 9, 18, 22, 28, 33, 37, 40, 41, 42, 43, 47, 50, 51, 52, 53, 54, 55, 57, 58, 59 (top), 60, 63, 64
Kenneth Coles: pp. 10, 11, 12, 26
Associated Press pp. 34, 39

Corel Professional Photos: pp. 4, 5, 48, 49, 59 (bottom), 62, 65
John Richards: pp. 17, 24

Dedication

For Tyler, best of luck in your racing career!
-SS

About the Author

Susan Sexton has always enjoyed reading books. She grew up reading mysteries, adventures, and biographies. As a child, her favorite book was *The Witch of Blackbird Pond*. Now Ms. Sexton is fulfilling a longtime dream—writing books.

Ms. Sexton taught elementary students for several years in Missouri. She enjoys reading, writing, and traveling. She also loves spending time with her husband and children and their pets—Tally, a golden retriever; Sammy, a cat; and Spikey, an iguana.

Text © 2003 by Perfection Learning® Corporation.
All rights reserved. No part of this book may be reproduced, stored in a retrieval system, or transmitted in any form or by any means, electronic, mechanical, photocopying, recording, or otherwise, without prior permission of the publisher.
Printed in the United States of America. For information, contact Perfection Learning® Corporation, 1000 North Second Avenue, P.O. Box 500, Logan, Iowa 51546-0500.
Tel: 1-800-831-4190 • Fax: 1-800-543-2745
perfectionlearning.com

PB ISBN-13: 978-0-7891-5884-0   ISBN-10: 0-7891-5884-1
RLB ISBN-13: 978-0-7569-1144-7   ISBN-10: 0-7569-1144-3

3 4 5 6 7 PP 15 14 13 12 11
PP / 06 / 11

Table of Contents

Introduction 5
Chapter 1 In the Beginning 7
Chapter 2 The Car 13
Chapter 3 Safety 27
Chapter 4 The Race 35
Chapter 5 The Famous 43
Chapter 6 The Young 51
Chapter 7 Getting Interested? 61
Glossary 65
Index 68

Introduction

Most people have heard the names Jeff Gordon and Tony Stewart. What do these famous **NASCAR** drivers have in common? They both have raced **sprint cars**. Indy drivers Mario Andretti, Johnny Rutherford, and A. J. Foyt also have raced sprints. And their experience in sprint car racing led to their successful Indy racing careers.

NASCAR and Indy racing have been popular for a long time. Many visitors fill the huge speedway stands to watch the famous drivers race. But sprint car racing is quickly growing all over the U.S. It is becoming a very popular sport because it's fast and exciting. And anyone over the age of five can race at some level.

Chapter 1

In the Beginning

Steve Kinser

One of the most famous names in sprint car racing is Steve "The King" Kinser. Steve has been considered the king of sprint car racing for many years.

Steve was born in Bloomington, Indiana, in 1955. He began his racing career in 1976.

Steve was a high school wrestler, so he was always in good physical shape. And he knows that's important in sprint car racing. Even now, Steve runs and plays racquetball during the off-season. Staying in good shape is part of the key to Steve's success.

A good driver must have the strength to muscle his or her powerful car around the track. Sprint car races are usually short. But the drivers must be able to **endure** the pressure and effects that racing has on the body.

Racing skill must run in the Kinser family. For quite a while, Steve's crew chief was his cousin, Karl. Karl and Steve teamed up from the very beginning of Steve's racing career. They were very successful.

Steve's son, Kraig, and Karl's son, Mark, are also successful racers. Steve's brother, Randy, and cousin, Kelly, race too.

In the World of Outlaws series, Steve has won over 400 **A-Main** events. He's won the Knoxville Nationals a total of 15 times. That's more than any other driver.

Steve's best year in sprint car racing was in 1987. He won a total of 56 races.

Steve's not just a sprint car racer. He has tried Winston Cup **stock car** racing and Indy car racing. But Steve has decided to stick with sprint cars. After all, he *is* The King!

Sprint Car History

Some people think that **open-wheel** racing is one of the oldest forms of racing. Many think that it's been around since the late 1800s. Sprint cars were modeled after those early open-wheel cars.

In the early 1900s, open-wheel drivers wanted to race their powerful machines. So they began racing their cars at fairgrounds—on horse racing tracks.

The fairground tracks were usually about 1 mile long. But some of the smaller fairgrounds had $\frac{1}{2}$-mile tracks. Open-wheel racing became very popular. Soon, some fairground owners changed the horse racing tracks into open-wheel racing tracks.

Some of these tracks are still used today. The Knoxville Raceway in Iowa is one. This track is where the Knoxville Nationals are held each year.

One of the first organizing bodies of open-wheel racing was the American Automobile Association (AAA). The AAA planned races all over the United States.

In 1915, state fairground managers formed the International Motor Contest Association (IMCA). Then many of the 1- and $\frac{1}{2}$-mile fairground tracks belonged to the IMCA.

As sprint car racing became even more popular, more sponsoring groups formed. Today, there are over 30 organizations dedicated to different types of sprint car racing.

Early sprint cars were called *big cars*. Big-car racing was very popular in the 1920s and 1930s. The drivers usually built their own cars. So the cars didn't all look the same.

There aren't many of the early sprint cars around today. But some can be found in old garages or barns.

Many people like **restoring** these old cars as a hobby. The restoration takes a long time. But when the car is finished, it's worth it. It looks brand-new.

Interest in big-car racing was at its highest in the 1930s. The cars were powerful. But they were also very dangerous.

The drivers' heads stuck up out of the cars. There were no safety features to protect them. The drivers were very brave to race those cars and risk injury or even death.

In the 1950s, **roll bars** were attached to all sprint cars. They were placed behind the drivers' heads. These bars extended above the drivers to protect them in case their cars rolled over.

1962, Eldora Speedway, USAC's first race
#1 Parnelli Jones, #5 Roger McCluskey,
#63 Johnny Rutherford
All are USAC sprint car champs.

In the late 1960s, **roll cages** were introduced. These frames surrounded the drivers to protect them even more.

The basic design of sprint cars has remained sleek and **aerodynamic**. Just the basic parts needed to drive are there. The bodies are just big enough to cover those few parts.

However, many improvements have been made. The materials used in building the cars have improved. Tires have also improved. And more safety features have been added.

As sprint car racing developed, other types of open-wheel racing did too. Indy cars, Formula One cars, and **midgets** also were created from early open-wheel race cars.

Would you believe that NASCAR even had a sprint car division in the early 1950s? However, it didn't catch on. So NASCAR went back to organizing just stock car races.

Today, sprint car racing isn't just popular in the United States. Racing groups can be found in Australia, New Zealand, and Canada. Paved-track races are even held in South Africa.

1958, Mt. Clements, Michigan
#70 Cotton Farmer from Texas
#71 Pete Folse from Tampa, Florida

Chapter 2

The Car

Jack Hewitt

Jack Hewitt was born in 1951 in Ohio. He is a sprint car legend who has been racing for many years. And there aren't any signs that he's going to quit.

Jack is tough to the core. And he has a very strong desire to win. Jack has won championships with the All-Star Circuit of Champs. He's also won with the United States Auto Club (USAC).

Racing is certainly in Jack's blood. He races **winged** and **nonwinged sprints**. Jack even races stock cars.

Jack is usually in front of the pack no matter what he's racing—and no matter where he's racing.

In one run of bad luck, Jack was injured. In the early 1990s, another driver lost control of his sprinter and landed on top of Jack's car.

But Jack's fighting spirit helped him through. He made a quick recovery, and before long he was back on the track.

It may be a while before Jack retires. Until then, watch for him to give the other drivers a run for their money.

The Parts of a Sprint Car

Today's sprint cars still have the same basic shape of the first sprinters. But most other things about the sprint cars have changed.

Safety features have been added. Strong but light materials are used to build the racers. And don't forget those wings!

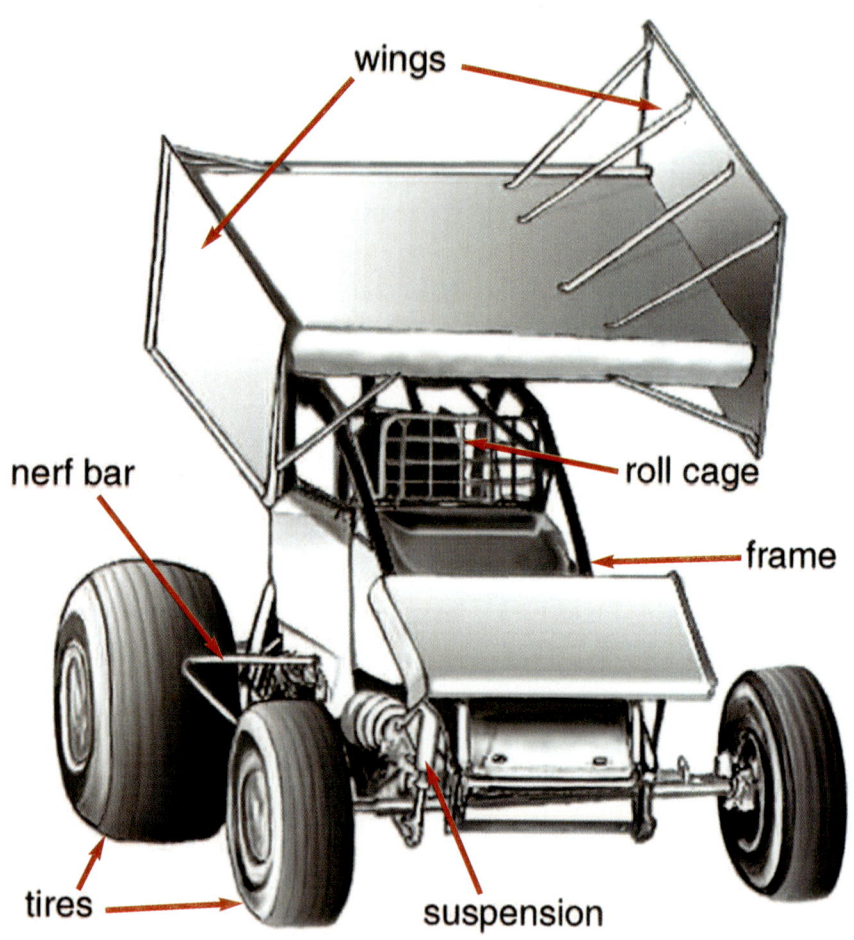

Sprint cars usually weigh less than 1,300 pounds, and that includes the drivers.

These race cars are very light. Some sprint cars have wings that force them down on the track. Then the drivers have more control.

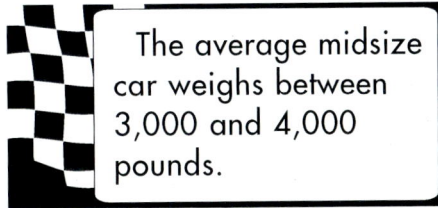
The average midsize car weighs between 3,000 and 4,000 pounds.

Types of Cars

Sprint cars fall into two main groups—winged and nonwinged. This means that one group of sprints has top and nose wings and the other does not.

Winged sprint cars don't really have wings like birds. Their wings are shaped like square, upside-down airplane wings.

The large 5-foot by 5-foot top wing is mounted to the roll cage over the driver's head. The top wing can be adjusted to different heights. It can also be adjusted to different angles.

On some cars, **mechanics** use tools to lock the top wing in place before a race. On other cars, the drivers have controls to adjust the wings during the race.

The 2-foot by 3-foot nose wing is attached near the front of the car between the front wheels. The height and angle of the nose wing are also adjusted before a race. It cannot be adjusted during the race.

When wings were first used, they were made of plywood. They didn't have the aerodynamic design of today's wings. But they still worked.

The purpose of these wings is to push the sprint cars down onto the track. The top wing pushes down with hundreds of pounds of force. This gives the tires better **traction** and drivers better control of the cars.

Many airplane wings are rounded on the top and flat on the bottom. They're also thicker toward the front. This shape is what helps airplanes rise into the air.

As an airplane moves forward there is a great amount of airflow around the wing. The air flows over and under the wings. The wings' shape causes the air under the wings to have the greater force. And since the force is pushing up, the airplane is lifted into the air.

But this idea is just the opposite for sprint cars. The tops of sprint car wings are flat. And the bottoms are rounded. When a sprint car moves forward quickly, the air flow is the opposite of the flow over airplane wings. There is more force pushing down on the flat sides, or tops, of the wings. This keeps the car down on the track.

Winged sprint car drivers think that their cars are safer than the nonwinged cars. The cars are easier to handle. And if a car tips over, the large wing helps cushion the blow to the driver.

Winged drivers are glad the large wings are there to help protect them. But they sure cost a lot to replace. A new wing costs between $500 and $600. Add that to the cost of the device that moves it, and the total cost is about $1,000.

Drivers aren't the only ones who like the top and nose wings. Sponsors like them too. The wings are like billboards. Car sponsors can put their names and logos on the wings. And the fans can see the sponsors' names over and over again as the cars circle the track.

Steve Kinser knows the cost of a new wing. As long as he's been racing, he's probably had to replace several. But then there was the time his wife ran over one.

On a cold night at the race track, Steve's wife and a friend were sitting in a truck. They decided to turn on the truck so they could have some heat. The truck was in gear. It lurched forward, and they accidentally ran over the wing.

The winged sprint cars may be the most easily recognized. But for many fans, the nonwinged cars are just as exciting.

Nonwinged sprint cars are more like the first sprints of the 1930s. Their body styles haven't changed much. These are like the cars that drivers such as A. J. Foyt, Parnelli Jones, and Johnny Rutherford drove in the 1960s.

Nonwinged sprint cars are more dangerous than the winged cars. The drivers don't have the protection from the large wings if the cars tip over. Also, the cars are harder to control.

Since nonwinged sprints are harder to control, the drivers go slower than those in the winged cars. Drivers don't always use the larger engines that the winged cars do.

But driving the nonwinged cars takes a lot of skill—probably more skill than driving a winged car. Since these cars are harder to control, the driver's reaction time must be quicker. A drivers' skills can mean the difference between winning and losing the race.

The Frame and Body

The **frames** may be light, but they are strong enough to protect a driver during a crash or rollover. The sprint car frames are made of steel and **molybdenum**. Using the two materials together in making the frame increases its strength.

The sprint car frames include roll bars and roll cages above the drivers.

Early sprint cars had heavy steel body parts. But today's sprinters have body parts made of lightweight fiberglass.

Fiberglass is really glass. But it's not in the same form as windows or drinking glasses. This glass is formed into very thin, fine strands. The glass strands are flexible. But they are much stronger than steel. And they won't burn or rot away.

> Glass is made from sand and other materials. These materials are heated in large furnaces so that they melt together. The melted glass then pours through very tiny holes at the bottom of the furnace.
>
> As the liquid flows through the holes, the melted glass cools and the strands are caught on spools. These strands are wound on the spools just like thread. As the spool winds, it stretches the strands even thinner. Some strands can be thinner than a human hair! Then the cooled strands are twisted or woven together to make many fiberglass materials.

Fiberglass is used in making car bodies. But it's also used for many other products, including insulation, cloth, and fishing rods.

"Nerf" bars are an important part of sprint cars. These bars are attached to the frame. They stick out from a sprinter and fill in the open space between the front and rear tires.

The nerf bars keep other sprinters from driving into the open space between the wheels. They keep cars from becoming tangled up at high speeds. The bars also give drivers added protection in accidents.

The working parts of sprint cars are pretty simple. And there aren't any extras on the cars. Drivers want their sprinters to be as light as possible. So the cars aren't loaded down with needless extras.

The Engine

Engines are probably the most important part of sprint cars. They are the power behind the cars. And that's what can win a race!

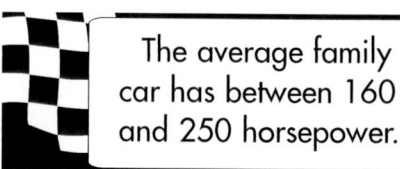

The average family car has between 160 and 250 horsepower.

The Super sprints use 410-cubic-inch motors. That size motor can pull up to 800 **horsepower**. And it means sprinters can reach speeds of 160 to 170 mph!

Most teams buy used, inexpensive motors. Then they work on the motors and replace worn parts to put them back in good condition. The best new motors can cost up to $35,000. So racers really take care of what they have.

A racing team takes an engine apart often—usually about every 6 to 12 races. They check each part for wear. Sometimes parts must be replaced.

The motor parts are cleaned before they're put back together. It can cost a lot of money to overhaul a motor. But when teams spend thousands of dollars for the motor, they can't afford to ignore problems.

Some drivers choose to race in the 360-cubic-inch engine class called Limited sprints. The 360-cubic-inch engines are smaller. They produce less horsepower than 410-cubic-inch engines and run a couple of seconds slower than the larger engines. But they cost less to build and maintain.

The wings on Limited sprints must be **fixed**. They can't be adjustable.

Even though Limited sprints are slower, they can be every bit as exciting to watch as the Super sprints.

For an even tighter budget, there are Econo sprint cars. The engines are 305 cubic inches. That means they have even less power than the Limited sprints. Econo sprint cars don't have nose wings.

The engine used by the Pennsylvania Four-Cylinder Sprint Car Association is even smaller. These are small, 4-cylinder engines.

For the new sprint car racer, driving a Limited or Econo sprint can save money. And the slower and less powerful cars can give new drivers much-needed experience before moving up to race with the "big boys," or more experienced drivers.

The Starter

Sprint cars must have running motors to race. But they don't start with keys like regular cars do. Instead, sprint cars need a push start.

When sprint cars need to move somewhere, they must be pushed. Most cars have a push bar on the back.

In the pit area, people on **four-wheelers** push the cars. That's how the sprinters can get to the lineup area or back to the pits.

When the sprinters are in the lineup area, they're ready to move onto the track. But they can't get there by themselves. Trucks, called *push trucks*, begin pushing the sprinters onto the track. The trucks push the cars at 20 or 30 miles per hour.

When the sprint cars' wheels begin to turn, other parts on the cars begin to move—even parts of the motors. And when the motor parts begin going fast enough, the motor fires and starts turning on its own.

The trucks then exit the track. They line up off to the side and wait for the next group of sprinters to race.

 Some people in sprint car racing have talked about adding starters to the sprinters. But the push start has been a tradition for a long time. And most people don't want it to change.

If there is a crash, or if a car's motor stops, a push truck moves into action. As soon as it can get to the stopped sprinter under a yellow flag, it pushes the car into the pits. Or the truck pushes it to get it started again. Then the race continues.

The Fuel

Sprinters need **methanol** fuel to power their motors. Methanol is a safer fuel to use than the gasoline used in street cars. Sometimes when cars crash, they catch fire. A methanol fire is easier to put out than a gasoline fire.

But there's a downside to methanol. It takes almost twice as much methanol as gasoline to power an engine. So sprint cars need large fuel tanks. They usually have 30-gallon tanks. Methanol is also more expensive than gasoline.

The Tires

The tires are another important part of sprint cars. The two front tires are used for steering. They're not needed for traction, so they're narrower than the rear tires. They are about 8 inches wide.

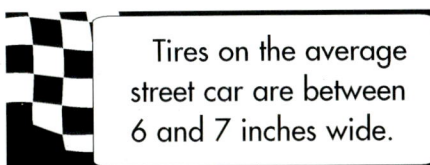

Tires on the average street car are between 6 and 7 inches wide.

The rear tires are much wider than the front tires and the tires on a street car. Sprint car rear tires can be 20 inches wide. And the right-rear tire is always wider and taller than the left-rear tire. These wide tires grab the track and push the cars around it.

The rear tires are mounted on the rear **axles**. The cars' powerful motors make the rear axles turn. The axle turns the tires to propel the car.

The rear tires push the sprint cars around the track with a great force. But since the tracks are left-turn-only ovals, the right-rear tires are the ones doing most of the pushing of the cars. Because of this, these tires wear out the quickest.

Crews change the right-rear tires more than the ones on the left. And some teams change the right-rear tires each time before the car goes onto the track.

On a left-turn-only oval, the cars are always turning left. Having the right-rear tire larger will make the sprint car go around corners easily and more naturally.

Consider a paper cup that is large at the top and small at the bottom. If you turn it on its side and roll it, the paper cup moves in a curved line, not a straight line. It is the same with a sprint car. A larger right-rear tire helps the car turn better around the curves.

Sprint car tires are inflated just like street car tires. But sprint car tires have much less air pressure in them—3 to 5 pounds. Sprint car tires are underinflated so more of the tires will touch the track during races. This provides more traction.

A small street car's tires will have from 28 to 32 pounds of pressure in them.

There are other things teams can do to help the tires do the best job. They can stagger the size of the tires. That means that they may put more air in some tires than in others. If the right rear tire is inflated more than the left rear, the car will go around corners better.

Crews can also use chemicals on the tires. Different chemicals make the tires harder or softer. The crews also make choices among different tire makers. They might choose from Goodyear, Hoosier, or McCreary tires.

The Suspension System

Sprint cars have powerful motors, large rear tires, and sometimes huge wings that put a lot of downward force on the tires. So how do the drivers control all that power? The cars have good **suspension** systems.

Even if the track is bumpy, good suspension will help keep all four tires on the track. In sprint cars, each tire has its own suspension. And so far, this setup seems to work best.

The Brake

Each sprint car has a single disc brake on the rear axle. But the drivers don't use the brake much during races, not even when they're sliding at top speed around the corners.

If the drivers apply their brakes too hard, there is a chance that their cars will **stall**. And that means a push truck would have to come help. The stalled car would then fall way behind the others in the race.

So instead of braking, drivers keep their foot on the gas and broadsail, or slide, through the turns. That's the way to win the race.

Smaller engine size, fewer parts, and a used car can help save money, especially for the weekend, local-track racer. But that doesn't mean the racing is less exciting.

Chapter 3

Safety

Jeff Gordon

Anyone who knows anything at all about NASCAR racing recognizes the name Jeff Gordon and his number 24. It was in 1991 that Jeff started racing stock cars. But in the '80s and '90s, he raced sprint cars.

Sprint car races are run on oval, dirt tracks. But a few races are run on pavement.

The sprint cars need to be set up differently for the two different tracks. The cars sit lower on a paved track and can go faster. And winged cars put their wings to the lowest position.

Drivers broadsail around the turns on a dirt track. But that's a big no-no on paved tracks. Sliding around the corners can cause bad accidents.

The track in Columbus, Ohio, is a paved track. The Columbus Motor Speedway features mostly stock car races. But once in a while, the winged sprint cars take to the track there.

Stock cars are usually much faster than sprint cars. And in the 1990s, the track record for stock cars was one lap in 14.56 seconds.

As fast as sprint cars can go on dirt, they are even faster on pavement. But in 1990, one young sprint car driver ran the Columbus oval even faster than the stock car record. He ran it in 12.43 seconds. And it was his first time on a paved track.

Would anyone ever guess that the driver was soon-to-be-NASCAR-winner Jeff Gordon? This four-time Winston Cup Championship driver was setting records back then too.

Driver Safety

Drivers wear special types of racing suits or jackets. These long-sleeved garments protect the drivers from rocks and car parts that might fly at them. The suits are thick, especially at the elbows, and they help prevent scrapes or more serious injuries if a car crashes.

The racing suits and jackets are fire-resistant. This means that they help protect the driver from burns if their cars catch on fire.

Racers must wear gloves. These protect their hands from flying objects. They also protect the hands during a crash or a fire.

Some drivers think that neck braces are a must. Neck braces keep the racers' heads from flopping around during a race. They also protect the drivers from neck injuries during crashes.

Drivers have to wear full-face helmets. New helmets are best. Wearing a used or worn helmet may not protect a driver as well, especially during a crash. The inside padding probably is shaped to the previous owner's head or the helmet might have a crack that can't be seen.

Helmets also protect the drivers' faces and eyes from flying objects, such as rocks, mud, and parts from other cars. Many drivers wear special fire-resistant hoods under their helmets too.

Car Safety

Arm restraints are important safety devices. If one car flips or crashes into another car, the force often causes the drivers' arms to flop outside their cars. The restraints hold the racers' arms inside. This prevents broken bones and other damage to the limbs.

All cars have roll cages. These are metal frames around the drivers' heads and shoulders. They protect the drivers in the event of crashes or rollovers.

Each car must have a four-point harness. This is a special type of seat belt. Four-point means that the belt buckles, or attaches, in four different places. This holds the driver firmly in the seat.

Four-point harnesses buckle above each shoulder and at the side of each hip. The four straps come together in the middle of the drivers' chests. These harnesses keep drivers in their seats during races and during crashes or rollovers better than regular seat belts.

Some drivers use five-point harnesses. These are the same as the four-point ones, except they also buckle between the legs.

The area where a driver sits is very small. The seat supports and protects the driver's head, neck, and back.

Firewalls also protect the drivers. These are metal plates between the drivers and the motors and fuel tanks of their cars. Firewalls are intended to protect the drivers from fuel spills, and more importantly, from engine fires.

Before each race, the crews check their cars completely. The safety equipment is inspected, and the steering and brakes are checked. A car must be in perfect working order before a race.

Communication

During races, track officials have to communicate with the drivers. So they use flags and hand signals. These forms of communication help the fans watching races know what's going on too.

The Flags

- **Green Flag**—A green flag means GO! The official starter waves the green flag to start the race. It is also used to start a qualifying or practice lap. The green flag is waved after a caution so the drivers know that the race has begun again.

- **Yellow Flag**—This means caution. The drivers must slow down. They are to remain in position and not pass other racers. The yellow flag is usually **thrown** because of a minor crash or spinout or because something is on the track. On a yellow flag, the **pace car** comes out and leads the cars slowly around the track.

When the track is ready for restart, one of the officials places a cone near the flag official's stand. The cone is about 1$\frac{1}{2}$ car widths from the outer edge of the track. When the cars pass this area on the track, they must pass between the cone and the outside of the track. This forces the sprint cars to drive single file. They must stay in the same order they were in when the yellow flag came out.

When the danger is gone, the pace car goes back into the pits. The cone is removed after all drivers have passed by as the green flag is thrown again.

- **Red Flag**—This flag means stop racing immediately. Some tracks have drivers wait on the track. But others want the drivers to go right to the pits. The red flag means that the track is too dangerous to race on. The weather may be bad. Or a car might be completely blocking the track after a major accident. The officials will decide when the race will continue.

- **White Flag**—When the official waves this flag, it means that there is one lap left in the race. It is waved until the leader gets ready to cross the finish line.

- **Checkered Flag**—The official waves this flag as the leader crosses the finish line and continues to wave it until all racers have finished the race.

- **Black Flag**—The black flag means that a driver has broken the rules. The flag is either pointed at the rule breaker or it is held next to a board listing the rule-breaking driver's car number. That car is supposed to go to the pits right away. A black-flagged driver who doesn't go to the pits may be disqualified. And he may lose points.

- **Blue or Blue/Yellow Striped Flag**—This flag is used for passing. If the flag is held still, it means that a faster car is coming up from behind. And the slower car will be lapped. If the flag is waving, it means that the slower car should move over. This will let the faster car pass and lap the slower car. Not all drivers like to move over for faster cars. They don't like being lapped. But if this flag is waved, the driver must move out of the way.

Common Hand Signals

- An official's finger is drawn across the throat. This means to stop and turn off the car using the on/off switch.

- An official's hands are held flat, pushing downward several times. This means slow down.

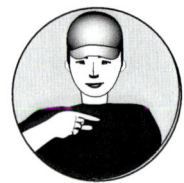

- The official's thumb and index finger open and close together. This means to give the car more gas.

- The official's finger is pointing toward the eyes. This means the driver needs to pay attention to the driving.

- The official's finger is pointing to the top of the head. This means that the driver's helmet is loose or missing.

Probably one of the most important safety factors is for drivers to learn the rules of racing. They need to know what they can do on and off the track and how they can be disqualified from a race if they don't follow the rules.

Chapter 4

Sarah Fisher in an Indy car

The Race

Sarah Fisher

Sarah Fisher was born in 1980 in Ohio. She has become a marvel in the racing world. She is the youngest driver ever to qualify and race in the Indy Racing League (IRL).

Sarah began racing at age five. Her parents, both racers themselves, started her in quarter midgets. When she was eight years old, Sarah began racing **enduro go-karts**.

Sarah won three World Karting Association (WKA) Grand National events by the time she was 14. And she won many other local and WKA-sponsored events too.

In 1995, Sarah began racing sprint cars—both 360s and 410s. She and her dad, Dave, teamed up to win. With just Sarah and Dave working on her sprint car, Sarah did well.

In 1998, Dave broke his arm. He couldn't rebuild the motors for Sarah's sprint car. So with Dave guiding her, Sarah rebuilt the motors herself!

Sarah's best sprint car finishes were in 1997 and 1998. She took second place at both the Pennsylvania Motor Speedway and the Eldora Speedway.

Then in 1999, Sarah was ready to move on. She and Dave felt that she needed some paved-track racing experience. She moved to midgets. Sarah won five different events in midget racing that year.

Sarah teamed up with Walker Racing in 2000. She began racing in the Indy Racing Northern Light Series (IRNLS). In April 2002, Sarah left Walker Racing.

In May 2000, Sarah made history. She became the third and youngest woman to qualify for the Indy 500.

There was a lot of pressure before the race. But Sarah knew that she had to stay focused and in good physical shape. She finished only 71 laps of the Indy 500 due to an accident. But she was okay. And she went on to compete in more IRNLS events that year.

Sarah Fisher definitely has a cool head and a good attitude about racing. She'll be one driver to watch in the future.

Two other female racers have raced in the IRL. Janet Guthrie was the first woman to race in the Indy 500 in 1977. And Lyn St. James won IRL rookie of the year in 1992 at the age of 45.

How a Sprint Car Race Is Run

Sprint car races almost always begin in the evening. First, the drivers take practice laps. The drivers use this time to get to know the track and see if their cars are working well.

Next each car takes turns running two qualifying laps. They usually run a warm-up lap, and then as the cars pass the flag official, they race around the track as fast as they can. The two qualifying laps are timed. The fastest lap is the one recorded for that driver.

After qualifying, the drivers are divided into heats, or racing groups. And the officials try to balance the heat by placing some fast and slow qualifying times into each heat.

There are usually four or five heats. The top four or five finishers from each heat then get to race in the main event. This is called the A-Main.

Before the A-Main event, there is usually a B-Main race. This race is for the sprint car drivers who didn't qualify for the A-Main event. It is usually as many laps as a heat.

The top two to four finishers of the B-Main are added to the A-Main. A total of 20 to 24 racers compete in the A-Main.

Officials arrange the sprint cars to make the races even more exciting. They take the top six qualifiers and line them up for the A-Main in reverse order. That means that the top qualifier will start in the sixth position. The driver with the sixth fastest time will start at the pole, or the first position.

Sometimes, sprint car-racing events last more than one day. In that case, more heats are run before the A-Main event on the last day.

Stock car races, like NASCAR, are much longer races than sprint car races. Stock car drivers have to go to the pit area several times during races. They may need more fuel or tires. Or they may need work done on their cars.

But since sprint car races are much shorter, drivers don't usually need to go in for gas or tires. But if there are many caution flags in a race, the cars may get low on fuel since the laps driven under the yellow flag aren't counted. So they may have to pit to fill up the fuel tank. Otherwise, the pits are usually just an area to work on cars between races.

What About the Fans?

For the fans, there are some things to remember on race day. The most important thing is to plan the trip to the track in advance. Then there's less chance of forgetting something.

Remember that the air sometimes cools when the sun goes down. A jacket might be needed. A backpack or bag can be used to carry the jacket and other items.

Take along some money. There will be a fee to get into the races. And you may become hungry or thirsty. Most tracks have stands where you can buy food and drinks.

Call the track or visit the track's Web site. Fans can get good information about what to expect on race day. Also, they can find out if they're allowed to bring food and water to the track, and if they can visit the pits before or after the races.

If fans can walk through the pits, they should get to the track early. There, they can see the sprint cars up close. And fans may get a chance to chat with the drivers. Sprint car drivers are often asked for autographs. So take along a pen or marker. The drivers sign shirts, photos, autograph books, or other keepsakes.

Cameras are also a must. Imagine having a photo taken with a driver who ends up famous in a few years.

Fans have a better view if they sit high in the stands. And on dirt tracks, there's less chance of getting sprayed with mud from the track, or hit with dirt clods!

Binoculars are a good thing to have at the track. It's fun to watch the drivers up close and see what the teams are doing in the pits.

Earplugs are important. The motors are very loud. And fans can damage their hearing after a while. So take earplugs along for protection. Most other fans will be wearing theirs too.

These suggestions will help make a trip to the races more fun.

Kindergarten students came out to the speedway as part of their Racing to Excellence program. Students who read books and received 60 points or higher on their reading test were given the opportunity to come to the speedway.

Other Types Of Open-Wheel Racing

Sprint car racing is also known as open-wheel racing or wheel-to-wheel racing. Since the tires aren't protected by fenders, they sometimes touch and scrape against other drivers' tires. They really do race wheel-to-wheel.

There are other types of open-wheel racing besides sprint cars.

Midget Racing

Midget-racing cars are another type of open-wheel race car. Like the sprint cars, the midgets also developed from the early open-wheel cars, such as the roadsters.

Midgets began as smaller versions of the 1930s "big" cars. The midgets were cheaper to build and race.

Racing midgets has grown into a popular sport, especially for drivers interested in getting experience. Midget drivers often move up to race with the drivers of NASCAR and Indy racing.

Midget racing started in 1933 in California. The races were fast and exciting. And they still are.

The races take place on shorter tracks, mostly $1/4$- to $3/4$-mile oval dirt tracks. Some races are on paved tracks. Midgets race on tracks in the U.S. and Canada.

Midgets, like sprint cars, don't have a lot of fancy additions. The drivers use the main parts to make the car go. They don't want the extra weight from unneeded items. That way, they can go faster.

The midgets are similar to sprint cars. But they are smaller and use smaller motors—usually 4-cylinder or V6 motors. The cars usually weigh about 950 pounds.

The midget drivers must wear fireproof safety gear, neck braces, and arm restraints.

The cars also have the same safety equipment as sprinters. This includes a strong roll cage and a five-point seat belt that is replaced every five years.

To find more information about midget racing, visit www.midgetracing.com on the Internet.

Midgets, like sprint cars, must be pushed to start. So push trucks are a big part of a midget race.

CART, IRL, and Formula One

CART, IRL, and Formula One cars are all very similar forms of open-wheeled racing. But each group has its own rules for the cars and motors. If you're interested in these types of open-wheeled racing, contact the individual organizations.

Chapter 5

The Famous

Danny Lasoski

Danny "The Dude" Lasoski was born in Dover, Missouri. Danny's love for and skill at racing sprint cars came from his father, George. George raced sprints on local tracks throughout Missouri.

Some may think that Danny's nickname was earned on the racetrack. But that's not so. His grandfather gave him that nickname when he was a baby.

Danny has been around racing his whole life. At age 20, he sold everything and teamed up with his dad. He won his first race at a local track in Marshall, Missouri.

Danny learned some important lessons from his dad. He learned that racing takes money. A person should have enough money to get to the track—but more importantly to get home from the track. In other words, a person shouldn't count on getting home using money won at the race.

Danny also learned that family is important. Racing shouldn't come before family members.

Another lesson he learned was to stay in good shape. Racing is hard on the body, so Danny keeps his body in top physical shape.

Danny has raced for a few different owners. But he is currently racing for Tony Stewart, a famous NASCAR Winston Cup driver. Tony used to be a full-time sprint car driver. He keeps his ties to sprint car racing by owning a car.

Tony and Danny met in the early 1990s. They were both racing sprint cars. When Tony moved on to stock cars, Danny stayed in sprint car racing.

Then in 2001, Tony asked Danny to drive for him. Danny agreed. And it looks like this partnership will last for a long time.

Racing is going well for the newly formed team. Danny won the World of Outlaws Knoxville Nationals in 2001. He beat 15-time winner Steve Kinser.

Keep looking for "The Dude" to win again! And again!

Those Famous Outlaws

Sprint car racing can be found in almost every state. There are different race sponsors. Probably the best-known sponsoring group is the World of Outlaws.

The World of Outlaws began in 1978. This group races all over the U.S. on dirt tracks. The races are often shown on television.

The "outlaw" reference dates back to the 1930s. An outlaw was a driver who did not belong to a club.

Many people recognize the names Steve Kinser, Sammy Swindell, and Craig Dollansky. They are members of the World of Outlaws. Mark Kinser and Andy Hillenburg are too.

World of Outlaws drivers race winged Super sprints. This means that the engine is the largest in sprint car racing—410 cubic inches.

The World of Outlaws holds their competitions at local dirt tracks. Big-name drivers come to town for the event. The local drivers who have Super sprint cars have the chance to race with these famous drivers.

When a race is just for local drivers, the winners usually take home trophies or small amounts of cash. But when the Outlaws come to town, there's more at stake.

The amount of money given out at a single Outlaws race can be tremendous. But that doesn't mean that the winner gets it all.

The total **purse** is divided among the winner, the second-place driver, and several other place finishers in the race. The winner takes the largest share.

That's pretty good money to win in one night. However, during an outlaw race, a local racer rarely sees much money.

It's the big-name Outlaws series drivers who win the money. It's almost like they swoop in, win the money, and move onto the next race in the series. It's as if they "rob" the locals of the chance to win a large sum of money. That's one reason why they're called the Outlaws.

Famous Tracks

Many tracks are just as famous as the drivers. Most drivers have favorite tracks. Maybe they've won there. Maybe they think they've done their best racing there. Or maybe they just like the tracks.

Eldora Speedway

Eldora Speedway is in Rossburg, Ohio. This track in the southeast part of the state is a $1/2$-mile, clay, high-banked, oval track. It is considered the fastest track that sprint cars run on.

Many drivers list Eldora among their favorite tracks. Exciting races run there often. The USAC holds events there. Events in which the World of Outlaws race take place there too.

The most popular event at Eldora Speedway is run by the All-Star Circuit of Champions. This special event is one of the races in the Ohio Sprint Speedweek.

In the Ohio Sprint Speedweek, there are seven different races. And each race is held at a different Ohio track.

Knoxville Raceway

The Knoxville Raceway is in Knoxville, Iowa. It is also a $1/2$-mile, clay, high-banked, oval track.

Many racers think that this track is the best in the country. There are 24,000 seats, and they're often filled, especially during the Knoxville Nationals.

The Knoxville Nationals is a four-day event that is attended by the World of Outlaws drivers and others. They come from the U.S. and from other countries. Thousands of fans come to watch the Knoxville Nationals too.

Right next to the racetrack is the National Sprint Car Hall of Fame and Museum. Visitors can learn about the history of sprint car racing. They can learn about famous drivers and races and see sprint cars on display.

Williams Grove Speedway

Another favorite track is the Williams Grove Speedway in Mechanicsburg, Pennsylvania. And it, too, is a $1/2$-mile, clay, oval track.

This track has a regular Friday night show. That's when the 410 Super sprints race.

The World of Outlaws races at this track seven times a year. And the USAC Midgets race here once a year.

The National Open is the most famous race at Williams Grove Speedway. Many of the famous drivers enter this race.

Silver Dollar Speedway

Many tracks can be found on the West Coast. The Silver Dollar Speedway is in the northern city of Chico, California. This track is a $1/4$-mile, clay oval.

The World of Outlaws holds a two- or three-day event at the Silver Dollar Speedway. Famous drivers, such as Sammy Swindell and Steve Kinser, have raced and won at this track.

The Gold Cup Race of Champions is held at the Silver Dollar Speedway. This race began as a 200-lap race. But since 1972, the race has only been 100 laps. That's a lot of driving around and around on a very short track.

More Famous Racers

Mark Kinser

The Kinser name is well known in the world of sprint car racing. Steve Kinser is a famous sprint car driver. His cousin, Karl, was Steve's crew chief for many years.

Mark Kinser is Karl's son. Mark races sprint cars too. And Mark's dad is now *his* crew chief.

Mark broke into sprint car racing at Indiana's Bloomington Speedway. It was the first sprint car race for the now third-winningest driver in sprint car history.

Mark has won over 140 World of Outlaws A-Main events. He's won two Outlaws Championships. And he's won the Knoxville Nationals three times.

Mark Kinser

A. J. Foyt

A. J. Foyt was born in 1935 in Texas. When people hear his name, they usually think of Indy cars. But A. J. actually began racing other types of cars, including USAC sprint cars.

A. J. is considered one of the best sprint car drivers ever. He won many races. But in 1964, he decided to race only Indy cars. He won the Indy 500 three times.

A. J. owns an IRL team now. So he is still involved with the sport of racing.

Mario Andretti

Mario Andretti was born in Italy in 1940. Many people recognize his name. He's a famous open-wheel driver. Mario began his racing career in nonwinged sprint cars.

Mario's family moved to the U.S. in 1955. His first race in the U.S. was in Pennsylvania, where his family settled. This is when Mario learned a lot about racing. Racing sprint cars was key in launching his racing career.

After racing sprint cars, Mario moved on to Indy cars. He won the Indy 500 in 1966. He holds 33 Indy car championship titles.

After Indy cars, Mario moved on to Formula One cars. He raced all over the world. And he won the World Championship in 1978.

Mario has raced sprint cars, Indy cars, Formula One cars, and stock cars—just about anything that can be raced.

Now Mario is retired from racing. He is a spokesman for racing, though. And he stays very involved in his son Michael's racing career.

Mario is one of the best racers of all time. People will remember his name for a long, long time.

Chapter 6

The Young

Sammy Swindell

Sammy Swindell was born in 1955 in Tennessee. He grew up watching his father race sprint cars. And at the age of 15, Sammy wanted to try it. In his first year of racing, Sammy won 11 main events.

Sammy studied physics and engineering in college. Racing sprint cars helped pay for school.

Soon, racing was taking too much of Sammy's time. If he quit racing, he couldn't afford to go to college. But he couldn't continue to do both. Sammy decided to focus his time and energy on racing. And for the three-time World of Outlaws champ, it was the right decision.

Sammy used his skills and knowledge from college, though. He always worked on his own car. The changes and improvements he constantly made to his car helped him become the leader and champ that he was.

Sammy has won over 240 A-Main events. And that places him right behind Steve Kinser.

Like Kinser, Sammy has also tried his hand at other forms of racing. He's successfully raced NASCAR stock cars and trucks. And he's raced Indy cars and other forms of open-wheel cars.

Sammy's racing success was the result of his attitude about life—be the best at whatever you do. Today, he is semi-retired and helping with his son's racing career.

Racing For Kids

Jeff Gordon is a famous NASCAR stock car driver. Jeff began racing go-karts and sprint cars at a very young age. He was lucky. His parents were interested in racing. And several racing programs were available for young children at the time.

The Quarter Midgets of America (QMA) sponsors racing for kids ages 5 to 16 years old. Quarter-midget racing began in the 1930s in the Los Angeles, California, area. Now groups can be found in all 50 states and Canada. In some places, children as young as $4\frac{1}{2}$ years old are learning to race. But they must be 5 years old to enter events.

The cars are called quarter midgets because they are only about $\frac{1}{4}$ the size of adult midget race cars, which are much smaller than sprint cars. The quarter midgets are about the size of go-karts.

Quarter-midget races are run on dirt tracks that are $\frac{1}{20}$-mile long. Quarter midgets can circle the track in 6 or 7 seconds. That's racing along at about 30 to 35 miles per hour (mph)—scary for some children. But for kids who want to learn to race, going fast is fun.

Age, weight, and type of motor divide the quarter-midget racing classes. A child's racing experience is important also, when being placed in a class.

Novice Class

New drivers are called *novices*. The younger novices are in the Junior Novice group. And the older novices are in the Senior Novice group.

The Junior and Senior Novice classes do not compete in races. Instead, the drivers learn about racing. It is a chance for new drivers to get the feel of a quarter-midget car and train to be better drivers.

The Novice class teaches new drivers what to do before, during, and after races. They learn how to line up for a race. They also learn how to pass other cars once a race is under way.

The class also teaches drivers how to drive on an oval track. The instructors usually set up cones around the track. The cones are placed in the corners and on the **straightaways**. The cones mark the path of the line, which is the fastest way around the track.

The students are told to drive on the outside of the cones on the straight part of the track and in between two cones on the corners. This helps new drivers see that they don't want to drive just on the **inside** of the track.

The fastest way around the track isn't always driving the inside, which is the shortest distance around the track. Driving the inside causes drivers to lose too much time on the corners. The best and fastest way is to follow the line of the track.

Racing Classes

Once a novice driver has participated in several **noncompetitive** "races," it's time to move on to another class. And this time, it is a *racing* class!

Drivers may move to the Honda Class. In this class, Honda motors are used. These engines must remain **stock**, or as they were when they were purchased new. They cannot be **souped up**. Honda motors are also less costly than other motors.

An experienced driver might want to move to the Stock Class. This is a class where other types of motors are used. And again, the motors must remain stock.

The drivers in the Honda and Stock Classes race in one of three divisions. The younger racers compete in the Junior Division. The older drivers race in the Senior Division. The Heavy Division is for drivers who weigh over 100 pounds.

Older drivers from ages 14 to 18 who have racing experience can move even higher. They can begin racing half-midget cars in the Junior Division.

Half-midget cars are $1/2$ the size of regular midgets. They're about twice the size of the quarter midgets.

Drivers who are 19 years old and older can race in half-midget cars too. They race in the Senior Division. And no matter how old the racers are, they can race half midgets for as long as they want to.

Cost of Racing

Quarter-midget racing is a safe sport for children. And that's the most important thing for parents. But parents also have to consider the cost of racing.

Quarter-midget cars cost money. A new car can cost up to $3,000. And a kit with a Honda motor can cost as much as $4,500. But parents on a tight budget may still be able to afford cars. Older, used cars can cost as little as $500.

In order to compete, drivers must join QMA. That costs $100. Drivers will probably want to join their local club too.

Each track charges pit fees on race day. The pit fees range from about $25 to $50. This gets a driver and team through the gates on race day.

Racing can be expensive. But parents willing to buy used equipment can help save costs.

Why Race?

Some people may ask, "Why should children learn to race cars?" The answers are the same as for any other sport in which children participate.

Quarter-midget racing teaches good sportsmanship. Drivers learn to respect others' skills and abilities. And they learn to respect other racers as people.

Racing also teaches responsibility. Drivers must be responsible for their cars. They also have to be responsible for getting everything ready to go to the races and for packing up when they're over.

Many children's racing organizations have anti-drug programs. Kids learn about the dangers of using drugs. These programs help kids make wise choices in their lives.

Racing increases coordination. Good hand-eye coordination and large muscle coordination are needed as drivers try to pass other cars and turn corners.

Drivers develop self-confidence through racing. As children learn about and practice racing, their skills will improve. Eventually, they may win a race. And winning is a great confidence booster.

But children will also lose races. Racing helps them learn to lose with dignity. Drivers, along with their teams, learn to accept defeat and begin planning how to do better in the next race.

Quarter-midget racing is a great family sport. Parents, grandparents, brothers, and sisters help out. And that makes racing a fun way to spend quality family time together.

The best part for kids, of course, is winning a race. Most of the time, winners receive trophies or medals. And at some special races, the winners receive savings bonds.

Three Grand National races are held each year—an East Coast National event, a West Coast National event, and a Dirt National event.

Some racetracks keep track of points throughout a season, just like the big-time racers. Drivers get points for winning a race. Others receive points for the place in which they finished.

Then at the end of the season, the points are totaled. The quarter-midget driver with the most points usually receives a special award, such as a jacket.

There are many rewards in quarter-midget racing—not just the thrill of winning. One of the most important is the chance to compete in a safe, healthy, family-oriented sport.

Chapter 7

Getting Interested?

Where to Go

Sprint car racing is very exciting for the drivers and the fans. In fact, just watching sprint cars race can leave a person breathless. If you are interested in racing a sprint car, going to the races is a good start.

At the track, you can watch the drivers zoom around the track. You can see the pit area where the teams work on the cars. You can also see how the races are organized.

Track visitors can sometimes go into the pit areas before or after the races. This is a good chance to see the cars up close. And visitors can usually ask drivers questions about racing.

Going to watch a race is probably the best way to learn about racing. But there are other ways to learn too.

The National Sprint Car Hall of Fame and Museum is in Knoxville, Iowa. Visitors can learn about the history of sprint cars. They also can learn about past and present drivers. Many interesting stories about people and events are available. The hall houses some of the first sprint cars, as well as current styles of sprint cars.

A public library or bookstore has books about sprint car racing. Sprint car magazines and other publications are available. The Internet has dozens of Web sites dedicated to the sport of sprint car racing, the teams, and the drivers.

Many organizations sponsor sprint car races and other open-wheel races. Each runs races for certain types of sprinters. And each group runs races in one or two states or a small region of the U.S.

Most of these groups have their own Web pages that post race schedules, race results, and point standings. They also tell about their organizations and give information about drivers.

For example, USAC sponsors nonwinged sprint car races. These are held in the eastern U.S. Their Web address is **www.usacracing.com**.

The USAC first began in 1955. They not only sponsor nonwinged sprint cars. But they also sponsor other types of open-wheel racing—midgets and three-quarter midgets.

Another sponsoring group is the Sprint Car Racing Association (SCRA). This group sponsors nonwinged sprint cars. They run races on the West Coast. Their Web address is **www.scra.com**.

The World of Outlaws is the only group that sponsors races throughout the entire U.S. They sponsor races for winged sprint cars. And their Web address is **www.worldofoutlawsracing.com**.

These are just a few of the many sprint car sponsoring groups. To find a group in a certain area, check the phone book. Look under the headings "auto racing" or "sprint cars." Search the Internet. Or look in books and other publications about sprint car racing.

Kids' Groups

The best way for kids to learn about quarter-midget racing is to watch a race. Watching other children of all ages race around a dirt track is a good way to get excited about racing and see how safe quarter-midget racing is.

To find a quarter-midget racing club, visit the QMA Internet site at **www.QuarterMidgets.com**. This site lists clubs throughout the U.S. Or call QMA at 1-800-OVAL CAR.

By visiting a club, parents and kids can meet other quarter-midget racers. Interested families should also visit the tracks.

Many clubs provide training programs for new and young racers. And some clubs even have everything kids need for racing—including cars.

Quarter-midget racing clubs encourage everyone in the family to take part in some way. Some family members can help work on the car. Others can work the snack bar or help with scoring the races. And the ones who are too little to help can just play around and have fun with other kids.

Sprint car racing is one of the most powerful forms of racing. The cars go very fast, so the races are exciting to watch.

Join in the thrill of racing. Watch for events on television. Or join a local group. Or just pack up and GO TO THE RACES.

Glossary

aerodynamic
designed to reduce air resistance, especially to increase fuel efficiency or maximum speed

A-Main
featured race involving the best drivers

axle
shaft under the body of a vehicle that connects a pair of wheels

endure
to tolerate

enduro go-karts
small road-racing vehicle in which the driver seems to be lying on his or her back

fixed
immovable or securely in position

four-wheeler
ATV or all-terrain vehicle. This motor vehicle is designed for use on rough, sandy, or marshy ground, as well as on roads. It usually has only one seat.

frame

underlying or supporting structure that consists of solid parts and has something built around or on it

horsepower

unit of power, usually used to measure the power of an engine

inside

in racing, the section of a track that is nearest the center of the track. It is the shortest distance around the track.

mechanic

skilled worker who is employed to repair and maintain vehicles

methanol

colorless, volatile, poisonous liquid that is used as a fuel and in antifreeze for motor vehicles

midget

front-engine, single-seat, open-wheel (see separate entry) racing car that is smaller in body and engine size than standard cars of this type

Glossary

molybdenum
very hard, silver-colored metallic chemical element used to strengthen steel

NASCAR
National Association of Stock Car Auto Racing

noncompetitive
participating in a sport not for the win or prize

nonwinged sprint
type of race car that does not have added equipment on the top and nose

open-wheel
referring to vehicles with no fenders

pace car
vehicle that leads the competitors in a car race through several laps before the start of a race or during a caution but does not participate in the race itself

purse
total sum of money offered as a prize or prizes

restoring
act of bringing something back to an earlier and better condition

roll bar
reinforcing bar across the top of a vehicle to protect the occupant if the vehicle overturns

roll cage
protective network of metal bars enclosing the driver of a race car

souped up
having made changes to a vehicle's engine to make it more powerful

sprint car
racing vehicle that is midway in size between midget racers and ordinary racers and is usually raced on a dirt track

stall
to stop working suddenly

stock
unchanged

stock car
relating to a standard passenger car that has been modified for professional racing

straightaway
part of a racing track that does not curve

suspension
system of springs and shock absorbers on a wheeled vehicle that reduces the impact of bumps and uneven running surfaces and gives the wheels better contact with the road

thrown
past participle of throw; in racing, to wave a flag

traction
friction between a moving object and the surface on which it is moving. Without this friction, the object cannot move.

winged sprint
type of race car that has equipment added to the top and nose to push the vehicle down on the track for better traction

Index

Andretti, Mario, 5, 49
Eldora Speedway, 45
Fisher, Sarah, 34–36
Foyt, A. J., 5, 17, 48
Gordon, Jeff, 5, 26–27, 52
Hewitt, Jack, 12–13
Kinser, Karl, 7, 47
Kinser, Mark, 7, 44, 47
Kinser, Steve "The King," 6–8, 17, 44
Knoxville Raceway, 8, 46
Lasoski, Danny "The Dude," 42–44
National Sprint Car Hall of Fame and Museum, 46, 61
Quarter Midgets of America (QMA), 52, 53, 54, 55, 56, 57, 58, 63
racing
    classes, 54–55
    costs, 16, 20, 56
    fans, 38–39
    flags, 30–31
    for kids, 52–58, 63
    hand signals, 32
    midgets, 39–41
Silver Dollar Speedway, 46–47

sprint car
    bodies, 10, 19
    brakes, 25
    communication, 30–32
    engines, 20–21
    frames, 18–20
    fuel, 23
    history, 8–10
    safety, 9–10, 19, 28–29
    starters, 21–22
    suspension systems, 25
    tires, 23–25
    tracks, 45–47
    types of, 15–18
    wings, 15–18
Sprint Car Racing Association (SCRA), 62
Stewart, Tony, 5, 43–44
Swindell, Sammy, 44, 50–51
United States Automobile Club (USAC), 13, 62
Williams Grove Speedway, 46
World of Outlaws, 7, 44–45, 62